Helping Children See Jesus

ISBN: 978-1-64104-008-2

DEATH: The Wages of Sin
Old Testament Volume 14: Numbers, Part 2

Author: Arlene S. Piepgrass
Illustrator: Vernon Henkel
Computer Graphic Artist: Nathaniel Wibberly, Yuko Willoughby
Typesetting and Layout: Morgan Melton, Patricia Pope

© 2018 Bible Visuals International
PO Box 153, Akron, PA 17501-0153
Phone: (717) 859-1131
www.biblevisuals.org

All rights reserved. No part of this publication may be reproduced, stored in a retrieval system or transmitted in any form by any means, electronic, mechanical, photocopy, recording or otherwise, without the prior permission of the publisher, except as provided by USA copyright law

RELATED ITEMS

To access related items (such as activities, memory verse posters and translated texts) please visit our web store at shop.biblevisuals.org and enter 2014 in the search box on the page.

FREE TEXT DOWNLOAD

To access a FREE printable copy of the teaching text (PDF format) in English or other available languages, enter S2014DL in the search box. Add the item to your cart, and use coupon code XTACSV17 at checkout. Once your order is processed you will receive an email with a link to the free download.

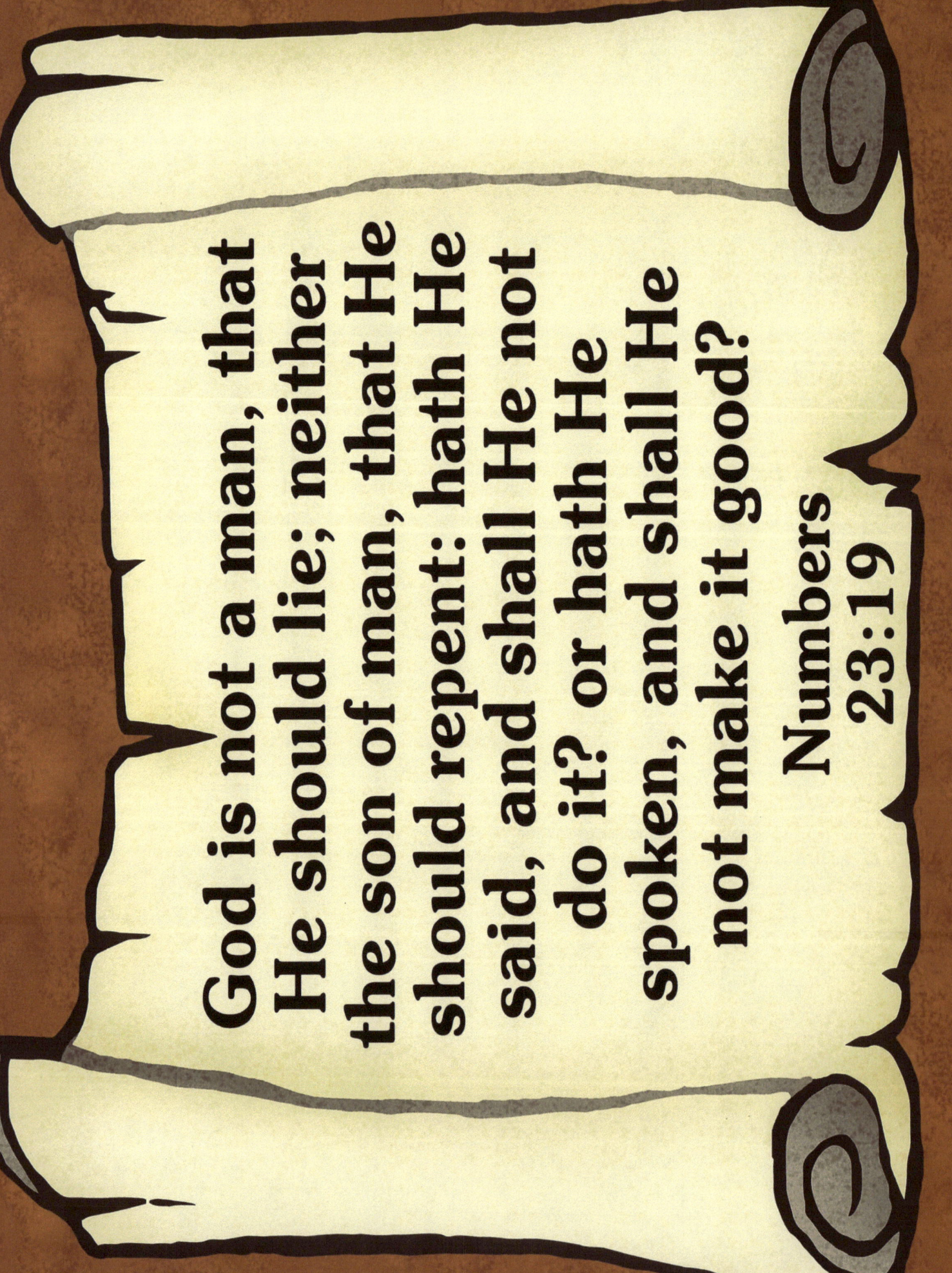

God is not a man, that He should lie; neither the son of man, that He should repent: hath He said, and shall He not do it? or hath He spoken, and shall He not make it good?
Numbers 23:19

Lesson 1
GOD'S INTOLERANCE OF THE SIN OF REBELLION

Scripture to be studied: Numbers 16-17

The *aim* of the lesson: To show that death is God's judgment for sin.

What your students should *know*: Rebellion against God is sin.

What your students should *feel*: Respect for the authority of God.

What your students should *do*: Submit to God's authority today.

Lesson outline (for the teacher's and students' notebooks):

1. Korah's rebellion (Numbers 16:1-30).
2. God's judgment (Numbers 16:31-50).
3. God's confirmation of His high priest (Numbers 17).
4. Our High Priest (Hebrews 5:5-10; 7:25).

The verse to be memorized:

God is not a man, that He should lie; neither the son of man, that He should repent: hath He said, and shall He not do it? or hath He spoken and shall He not make it good? (Numbers 23:19)

(*Teacher:* As you teach the memory verse, emphasize that the answer to the question is "Yes, God will do what He promises."

NOTE TO THE TEACHER

These events in the history of Israel are not recorded simply for information. They are given as examples and warnings for us. (See 1 Corinthians 10:11.) Pray that the Holy Spirit will teach you spiritual lessons for your own life. Then apply the lessons to the lives of your students.

God says, "The wages of sin is death" (Romans 6:23). This truth is vividly illustrated in the chapters of Numbers which we shall study in this volume. The Israelites repeatedly rebelled against God. They rebelled against His authority, His leaders, His provision and His direction. The *punishment* for their rebellion was death. The *remedy* for their sin of rebellion was repentance: returning to trust in God and obeying Him.

In our lesson today, we have the record of Korah's rebelling openly against God's appointed high priest. God showed that Aaron alone had been appointed to the priesthood. Any who dared to intrude into this office would be killed.

Today many false leaders present themselves as gods. They claim to be worthy of trust and implicit obedience. They reject and rebel against God's Son, the only way to God (John 14:6). God's judgment for such rebellion is eternal death.

THE LESSON

What do you think of when you hear the word *death*? (Encourage discussion. Death is separation, sorrow, weeping, end of life, loneliness, etc.) Death is not a happy time. But (with the exception of believers who are alive when the Lord Jesus comes) everyone will die one day. (See Hebrews 9:27.)

When did death begin? (Review briefly Adam and Eve's sin of disobedience. Emphasize that death was God's punishment for their sin. Explain that physical death is separation of the soul from the body. Spiritual death is separation of the person from God.)

Many years after Adam sinned, another man rebelled against God's authority.

Numbers 16:1-30

In the camp of Israel was an important man named Korah. He belonged to the tribe of Levi. As a Levite, where would his tent be located? (Near the tabernacle.) Why would he live close to the tabernacle? (The Levites were not priests. But they were chosen by God to help Aaron and the priests in the service of the tabernacle.)

Korah belonged to the family of Kohath. Do you remember what special work was assigned to the Kohathites when the tabernacle was moved? (They carried on their shoulders the furniture of the holy place and the most holy place.)

Korah was not allowed to enter the holy place and the most holy place until all the furniture was covered. He watched Aaron and his sons go in to do this. He should have been thankful that God had chosen him to serve in such an important work. Instead, he became jealous of Aaron and his sons, who were the only priests. He not only wanted to be a priest, but the high priest!

Korah went from tent to tent to stir up the people against Moses and Aaron. First he went to the tents of Dathan and Abiram. "We have as much right to serve as priests in the tabernacle as Aaron and his sons have," said Korah haughtily. "God said we are all holy. Why should Moses and Aaron be telling us what to do? We do not need them."

"You are right," agreed Dathan and Abiram. "We will join you against those men. Why should we listen to them? We are as good as they are."

As Korah went from tribe to tribe, the leaders listened to him. They nodded their heads in agreement. They talked to their families and made them dissatisfied.

Show Illustration #1

One day, Korah and 250 important Israelite leaders (called princes) went to Moses and Aaron.

"You have taken on yourselves too much responsibility," said Korah proudly. "We are just as holy as you are. We have as much right to serve as priests in the tabernacle as you do. What right do you have to lift yourselves up to such a high position?"

Can you think of anyone else who criticized Moses? What happened to that person? (Review Lesson 3, Volume 13–Miriam was covered with leprosy.) Korah knew this. Do you think he should have been afraid to accuse God's leaders?

Moses asked, "Korah, is it a little thing to you that God has chosen you from among all the Israelites to serve Him? Why are you not content with what God has given you to do? You are able to come closer to God than all the other people. Why do you want to be the high priest? What has Aaron done to make you dissatisfied with him?"

Korah answered, "We are all holy. We all have the right to enter the holy place and the most holy place."

Did they have that privilege? No. Only the one appointed by God had that right. Did Aaron choose to be the high priest?

– 19 –

(See Exodus 28:1.) No. God chose him. No man had the right to choose himself. (See Hebrews 5:4.)

Moses asked, "Where are Dathan and Abiram? Tell them to come here!"

"Why should we come?" they asked. "You brought us out of Egypt, where everything was nice, to kill us in this terrible wilderness. You have not kept your promise to bring us to a wonderful country where we would have plenty of fields and vineyards. Now you want to be king over us. We refuse to obey you!"

What was wrong with their answer? (1. Egypt was a place of slavery and misery. 2. God, not Moses, led them out. 3. God wanted to lead them to a good land but their unbelief barred them–at Kadesh-Barnea, Numbers 14:4. Moses did not want to be king; he was appointed leader by God.)

"Korah," Moses said firmly, "you and your 250 princes come here to the door of the tabernacle tomorrow morning. Bring your censers with incense to offer before the Lord. Aaron will be here, too, with his censer. Then God will show us whom He has chosen as His high priest."

Korah and his friends returned to their tents. Would they think about what they had done? Would they be afraid of what God might do to them? Would they repent and ask Moses and Aaron to forgive them?

NO! The Bible says they went home and tried to stir up more people against Moses and Aaron. The next morning Korah and the 250 princes boldly came to the entrance of the tabernacle. Many others gathered to see what would happen.

2. GOD'S JUDGMENT
Numbers 16:31-50

Before Moses or Aaron could say anything, God Himself took charge. He commanded, "Moses and Aaron, get away from these people. I am going to destroy them all in an instant!"

God had the right to destroy them. This is what they deserved. They were really rebelling against Him for He had chosen Aaron to be the high priest. If we had been in Moses' place, we probably would have said, "Go ahead, Lord, destroy them. I am tired of their grumblings and criticisms!"

But Moses and Aaron both fell to the ground on their faces begging God to forgive the people. "O God, must all the people die because of the sin of one man?"

God heard their prayer. Instead of giving the people what they deserved, He said, "Moses, tell the people to get away from the tents of Korah, Dathan and Abiram."

Immediately Moses shouted, "Quick! Get away from the tents of these wicked men or you will be destroyed with them! If these men die natural deaths, you will know they are right and God has not appointed Aaron and me to lead you. But if God performs a miracle and opens the ground to swallow them and all their belongings, then you will know that these men have rebelled against God."

Show Illustration #2

That moment, the earth split wide open. And these men, their tents and their families fell screaming into the opening. All were killed at once as the earth closed over them! God's judgment for their rebellion was *death*.

The other Israelites ran away screaming, "Let's get away from here before the earth swallows us, too!"

Then the Lord sent fire which killed the 250 princes. He told Eleazer, the priest, to take their censers and beat them into a big sheet of metal. With it, he was to cover the brazen altar in the courtyard.

"This will remind the people that no one may serve as a priest in My tabernacle unless he is appointed by Me," God said. "If anyone tries, the same thing will happen to him that happened to Korah today."

What a sad day in the camp of Israel! Do you think that the people repented and obeyed God? Do you think they were grateful that God had spared them when they, too, deserved to die? No! The very next morning some again accused Moses and Aaron, saying, "You have killed the Lord's people. You are responsible for those who died." Many joined them making a huge, noisy crowd.

When God heard them, He commanded, "Moses and Aaron, get away from these people. I am going to destroy them all."

Again Moses and Aaron fell on their faces and begged for mercy. But God had already started to kill them with a plague. Moses shouted, "Aaron, hurry and get some fire from the altar of sacrifice. Put incense on the fire. Carry it quickly among the people so they may have cleansing for their sins!"

Aaron stood between an angry God and sinful people, pleading for Him to spare them. God heard Aaron's prayer and withheld further judgment upon His people. But not before 14,700 had died! Think of this–almost 15,000 Israelites died because Korah wanted to be God's high priest in place of Aaron! If Aaron had not interceded for them, they all would have been killed.

3. GOD'S CONFIRMATION OF HIS HIGH PRIEST
Numbers 17

God said, "Moses, I am going to settle once for all the question of Aaron's priesthood. I am going to stop the continual murmuring of the people against you and Aaron."

Moses listened carefully to God's instructions. Then he explained to the Israelites what God commanded them to do.

"God is going to make clear whom He has chosen as His high priest. The leader of each tribe must put his name on a rod (dry stick) and bring it to the tabernacle. There will be 12 rods in all. I shall put Aaron's name on the rod for the tribe of Levi," Moses explained.

The 12 leaders did as Moses told them. When they came to the tabernacle, Moses continued, "God commanded me to put your rods in the most holy place in front of the ark of the covenant. He said He will cause one rod to produce buds overnight. The name of the man on that rod is the one He has chosen to be our high priest."

Moses followed God's orders and all returned to their tents. The next day Moses brought the 12 rods from the tabernacle to the leaders who were waiting expectantly.

Show Illustration #3

They couldn't believe their eyes! For Aaron's rod not only had buds, it had blossoms and ripe almonds hanging on it. In one night that dry stick had grown the way a living branch would have grown in a whole season. The rest of the rods were still dry sticks. There was no mistake. Aaron was God's choice!

4. OUR HIGH PRIEST
Hebrews 5:5-10; 7:25

Only Aaron, God's chosen high priest, could offer sacrifices which would satisfy God's holiness and obtain forgiveness for the people. Korah could not. Abiram and Dathan could not. Moses could not. God showed the people they could not stand before Him without Aaron. They died when they tried.

Show Illustration #4

We cannot stand before God alone either. We all deserve to die because of our sins. But God has provided a way for us to live. He has appointed His only Son, the Lord Jesus Christ, as our High Priest. With His blood He satisfied God's holiness and made it possible for God to forgive our sins. He stands between us and God.

Today there are many people like Korah. They say there are other leaders just as good as Jesus. (Muhammad, Buddha–name other religious leaders which the people in your area follow.) They say that by following them we shall go to Heaven. When the founders of these religions die they stay dead. God's Son, the Lord Jesus Christ, arose from the dead. This is God's proof that Jesus Christ is the only High Priest whom He has chosen. (See Romans 4:25; Hebrews 7:25; Acts 4:12.) The dead stick budded to become a type of the risen Christ.

Just as God destroyed Korah and those who rebelled against His chosen priest, Aaron, so He will again destroy those who rebel against His Priest, the Son of God. (See Revelation 20:14.)

Remember, "The wages of sin is death, but the gift of God is eternal life through Jesus Christ our Lord" (Romans 6:23). (*Teacher:* Review memory verse to emphasize that God will do what He says in His Word.)

Lesson 2
GOD PROVIDES A SUBSTITUTE FOR THE SINNER

Scripture to be studied: Numbers 21:1-9

The *aim* of the lesson: To show that God provided a way to escape death (which is His judgment on sin).

What your students should *know*: That God has provided a Substitute to die in our place.

What your students should *feel*: Utterly unable to help themselves.

What your students should *do*: Believe on the Lord Jesus Christ and live.

Lesson outline (for the teacher's and students' notebooks):
1. The hopeless condition of the Israelites (Numbers 21:1-7).
2. God provides a Substitute (Numbers 21:8-9).
3. The condition of deliverance (Numbers 21:8-9).
4. The brazen serpent: a type of Christ (John 3:1-18).

The verse to be memorized:

God is not a man, that He should lie; neither the son of man, that He should repent: hath He said, and shall He not do it? or hath He spoken and shall He not make it good? (Numbers 23:19)

> **NOTE TO THE TEACHER**
>
> The Lord Jesus said that the brazen serpent of Moses' day was a preview (some 1,500 years beforehand) of His death on the cross as our Substitute. (See John 3:14.) When Adam and Eve disobeyed God, death entered the world as God's judgment against sin. Instead of putting Adam and Eve to death, God killed a lamb as their substitute.
>
> All through the Old Testament, God teaches that He judges sin by death. But He has always provided a substitute to die in the place of the sinner. If He had not, the whole human race would have to suffer in eternal hell. By looking to Jesus, our Substitute (accepting His salvation by faith), we have eternal life.
>
> This account of Israel and the brazen serpent was written for our learning so that we may have certainty. (See Romans 15:4.)
>
> Use the map on the back cover when you mention the names of places.

THE LESSON

Almost 40 long years had gone by since the Israelites left Egypt. Nearly 38 years had passed since that sad day at Kadesh Barnea when they could have entered the land of God's promise. (Use questions to review the wrong decision Israel made at Kadesh Barnea and the consequences of their decision. See Old Testament Volume 13, Lesson 4.)

What were the Israelites doing those 38 years?
1. They were like prisoners wandering in the desert, going nowhere.
2. Day after day they buried those who died. More than two million people had to die before they could enter the land God promised them. Everyone who was over 20 years of age at Kadesh Barnea had to die for refusing to enter the land. (See Deuteronomy 2:14.) This meant over 1,000 died each week!

Does this sound like a happy time? No! Disobedience *never* makes people happy. Death was all they had to look forward to. As they sat in the doors of their tents, they must often have said, "If only we had obeyed God, we could now be enjoying the land of Canaan." What sad words!

BUT God still loved them. He chastised them–but kept His promise.
1. He did not leave them, even though they disobeyed Him (Deuteronomy 2:7).
2. He continued to send manna every morning (Deuteronomy 8:2-6).
3. He provided everything they needed (Deuteronomy 2:7).
4. Their clothes did not get old (Deuteronomy 29:5).
5. Their sandals did not wear out (Deuteronomy 29:5).
6. Their feet did not swell from walking in a hot desert (Deuteronomy 8:4).
7. He provided water from the flinty rock. God continued to be faithful!

How gracious God was to Israel! And He is the same today. (See Hebrews 13:8.)

Finally, the adults that left Egypt were dead. Their children, now grown, were the leaders. Other children were born in the wilderness. The number of people grew until there were as many as when they left Egypt.

Moses was still leading the people. Joshua and Caleb, the two faithful spies, were still alive. But Aaron (see Numbers 20:28) and all the other adults who had come out of Egypt were dead.

The Israelites were almost at the southern border of Canaan, the land God had promised them. All they had to do was get through a little country called Edom. Then they would be in the land God was giving them. But the king of Edom said, "No, you may not go through my land. If you do, my army will fight you. You had better not try it!"

So the Israelites had to take a longer route. They were tired. They were disappointed. They were discouraged. They began to complain–just as their parents had done. They forgot how much God hated complaining. They forgot that God had punished their parents because of their complaints. (See Numbers 11, 12; Old Testament Volume 13, Lesson 3.)

1. THE HOPELESS CONDITION OF THE ISRAELITES
Numbers 21:1-7

Show Illustration #5

"Why have you brought us up out of Egypt to die here in the wilderness?" they asked Moses defiantly. "Why are you leading us this way? It is too rough and hard."

Who was really leading them? (God, through the cloud by day and pillar of fire by night.) Does it sound as if they were thankful for all God had done for them the past 40 years?

It is true that the way was difficult. It is true that many died in the wilderness. But *why* did so many die? (*Teacher:* Let students respond.) It was their own fault. They were paying the consequences of their disobedience.

Some grumbled, "There is no bread to eat here."

"I am sick of this manna we gather every morning," another growled.

"We're always thirsty and there's no water around here," mumbled others.

"You said God was giving us freedom in a good land," others said with a sneer. "Is this what you call freedom? Is this what you call a good land?"

How hateful and ungrateful these people had become! They were acting exactly as their parents had. In speaking against Moses, they were really complaining against God. Speaking against God is a terrible sin.

God heard them. This time He punished them for their sin by sending fiery serpents (snakes) among them.

The snakes bit the people. Their bites were poisonous. Children were bitten; old people were bitten; parents were bitten. How frightened everyone became! Snakes were everywhere. The people could not get away from them. They could not kill them.

Screams were heard all over the camp. "OHHHHH! I've been bitten! I'm dying! Help me!"

Others tried to help those who were bitten. But the pain grew worse. In every tent there were the moans and cries of the dying.

Every day more people were bitten. Every day more people died. What a price to pay for their sin–DEATH!

The people could not help themselves. Their condition was *hopeless*! Soon they would all be dead! What could they do?

2. GOD PROVIDES A SUBSTITUTE
Numbers 21:8-9

If you had been one of the leaders of Israel, what would you have done? (Encourage discussion.)

They needed help. They knew, too, that God had sent the snakes. And they knew why He had sent them.

Going to Moses, the people admitted, "Moses, we have sinned. We have complained against you. We have complained against God. We were wrong. We are sorry for our sins. Please pray to God for us. Ask Him to forgive us. Pray that He will take away these dreadful snakes!"

Moses did pray to God for the people. Do you think God would answer such a prayer? Why? (*Teacher:* Encourage discussion. God sees when people are truly sorry for their sins and He forgives them. See Psalm 6:9; 51:17; 1 John 1:9. And God made a way to save these people.)

"Moses, make a serpent (or snake) out of brass," God commanded. Why brass? In the Bible, brass is a reminder of God's judgment. The brazen serpent was a picture (or type) of God's judgment of sin.

"It must look like the snakes in the camp," God continued. "Put the serpent of brass on a pole. Stand the pole in the center of the camp where all can see it."

Show Illustration #6

Moses followed God's instructions exactly. As the people watched, they might have been thinking, *Why is Moses doing this? How can a brass serpent help us? Why doesn't he pray that God will perform a miracle? Why a brass snake?*

3. THE CONDITION OF DELIVERANCE
Numbers 21:8-9

Moses gathered the people together. Pointing to the brazen serpent on the pole, he said, "God has sent help. When any of you are bitten, LOOK at the brass serpent and you will be healed immediately. You will not die. You will live. God has provided this to heal you. There is no other cure. Trust God. Believe Him. Obey Him. What God says is true. He cannot lie."

Show Illustration #7

Some asked, "Moses, are you fooling us? How can that serpent of brass do anything for us?"

Moses answered, "I do not understand *how* it can heal you. I only know that God said anyone would be healed *if* he *looked* in faith at the serpent. There is *no* other way. God has made it easy for you. Even your little children can be healed if they will LOOK at the brazen serpent."

Do you suppose all the Israelites immediately looked at the serpent? Or, since they were like people today, could something

– 22 –

like this have happened in the camp? A husband is bitten. His wife begs, "Please look at the brazen serpent."

"That is ridiculous!" her husband answers. "How can looking at that serpent heal me? Help me walk over to the tabernacle. Maybe the priest can help me."

Do you think he was healed by the priest? The husband died. He refused to follow God's way.

In another tent a moaning child tosses on her bed. Tenderly her mother carries her to the door of the tent. Urgently she commands, "Honey, hurry and look at the brass serpent so you can be well."

"You look for me, Mama," the girl pleads. "I am too sick to look."

"No, dear, I cannot look for you. You yourself must look at the serpent to be healed."

Lifting her eyes, the sick child gazes at the serpent of brass. Immediately she is well. She runs outside, playing as before. Just as God had promised, she was healed.

ALL who looked were healed. ONLY those who looked were healed. EVERYONE who refused to look died.

All the Israelites deserved death. But, because God loved them, He provided a remedy so they could live.

4. THE BRAZEN SERPENT: A TYPE OF CHRIST
John 3:1-18

One night, almost fifteen hundred years later, Nicodemus, a religious leader of the Jews, came to Jesus. He wanted to know how he could have eternal life.

"Nicodemus, you remember how Moses put a brass serpent on a pole in the camp of Israel," Jesus said.

Show Illustration #8

Nicodemus nodded. He knew well the history of the Jewish people. "That is a picture of Me, Nicodemus," Jesus explained. "I too will be lifted up [on a cross]. If you will 'look' at the cross, believing I died for you, you will have eternal life."

(*Teacher:* Make very clear that "look-ing" means obedience to the Word of God; faith in the provision of God; accepting by faith the salvation which Christ's death affords us.)

When the Lord Jesus died on the cross, do you think Nicodemus remembered his conversation of that night three years before? (See John 19:39.)

"LOOK to the cross [accept God's salvation] and LIVE" is God's only remedy for your sins. If you will receive His salvation, you will have everlasting life. If you sin by refusing to turn to the Saviour, the Lord Jesus Christ, you will suffer punishment forever. The wages of sin is *eternal* DEATH.

God helped the people of Israel. He provided the serpent of brass so they could escape death. God has help for you, for me. He has lovingly provided His Son as our Substitute. He, Christ Jesus the Lord, took the punishment we deserve for our sins. By trusting in Him, we will escape eternal death.

Many today are trying to come to God their own way. They think they will be saved by joining church, offering sacrifices, making vows, revering men. These may be good. But nothing we can do will save us. We are saved by faith in Christ alone. After placing all our trust in Him, we will then want to do good things.

In Old Testament days, God said to the Israelites, "Look unto Me and be ye saved, all the ends of the earth: for I am God, and there is none else" (Isaiah 45:22). In the New Testament we have the words of God's only Son, the Lord Jesus: "I am the way, the truth, and the life; no one comes to the Father, but by Me" (John 14:6).

Let us repeat our memory verse. God means what He says. He will do what He has promised.

The Lord Christ died on the cross in *your* place. Today, will you *look* to Him to save you? If you will truly believe that Jesus, the Lamb of God, took the punishment for your sins, you will live forever. If you have placed all your trust in Him today, will you please tell me so after class?

Lesson 3
THE HIGH PRICE OF SELF-WILL

NOTE TO THE TEACHER

The New Testament record associates Balaam with false teachers: "The way of Balaam" (2 Peter 2:15) is a reminder that he did religious work for personal gain. "The *error* of Balaam" (Jude 11) was his deceit and covetousness. "The *doctrine* of Balaam" (Revelation 2:14) was his attempt to corrupt God's people through worldliness. He encouraged them to live like the world instead of being separated as God commands.

Balaam and the Israelites vividly picture the truth of Proverbs 14:12: "There is a way which seems right to a man, but the end thereof are the ways of death."

As God allowed Balaam to have his own way, so He sometimes allows us to have our own way. Our self-will always displeases God and causes Him to withhold His blessing from us.

God hated Israel's being involved with the idolatrous Moabites. Likewise today, He despises worldliness in the lives of Christians (James 4:4). He admonishes us to be holy (1 Peter 1:15-16).

Covetousness has always been a snare. God knew it would be a great temptation and repeatedly warns us to set our affections on heavenly things, not on earthly gains.

For variety of teaching, work with your students outside of class so they can dramatize this lesson.

Balak was frightened! He was really worried! Who was Balak? He was the king of Moab. (*Teacher:* Indicate Moab on map.)

King Balak was worried and frightened because of the alarming news reports that came to his palace.

"SIHON HAS BEEN KILLED BY THE ISRAELITES."

Balak thought, *Sihon is king of the Amorites. He is strong! His army defeated us in battle.*

"THE LAND OF THE AMORITES POSSESSED BY ISRAEL."

To his aides King Balak said nervously, "The Amorites are just north of us. If the Israelites are occupying the land of the Amorites, they will soon move down and try to take Moab, too."

"OG, KING OF BASHAN, FIGHTS ARMIES OF ISRAEL."

Breathing a sigh of relief, King Balak thought, *Good! Og is even stronger than King Sihon. Og is a giant.* (See Deuteronomy 3:11.) *He will defeat the Israelites and take them away from my borders!*

"BASHAN FALLS TO ISRAEL. KING OG AND ALL INHABITANTS ARE DEAD."

1. KING BALAK HIRES BALAAM
Numbers 21:21-35; 22:1-20

Show Illustration #9

Now Balak was really alarmed. Calling his aides together, he said, "We are in real trouble. We will be no match for these Israelites. I cannot understand how they have defeated these powerful armies. Unless . . ." King Balak sat thinking. "Yes, this must be it. Their God is more powerful than our gods. Ummm. I know what I shall do. Listen carefully. There is a man far to the north of us in Mesopotamia. (Indicate on map.) His name is Balaam. He has power to bless people and to curse them."

King Balak commanded, "Go to Balaam and tell him about our trouble. Ask him to come and curse these Israelites. Take plenty of money along to pay him for his services."

It was a long journey to Mesopotamia. When King Balak's messengers arrived at Balaam's house, he invited them in.

Balaam listened to their request. When he saw all the wealth they were offering him, he thought to himself, *I would really like to go with them. I am flattered that King Balak thinks I am so powerful. I guess I really am important. I would like to have the money, but I am not sure God will let me go.*

To the king's aides he said, "You spend the night with me. The Lord will tell me whether or not I may go with you. I will give you an answer in the morning."

Do you think God would let Balaam go to Moab and curse His people, the Israelites? (Let students discuss, giving reasons for their answers.)

Five hundred years before this, God had given Abraham a special promise. He said, "I shall bless those who bless you, and curse anyone who curses you" (Genesis 12:3).

While King Balak's messengers slept, God spoke to Balaam. "Do not go with these men!" he said. "You must *not* curse these people. Remember–I have blessed them!"

When morning came, Balaam told the king's messengers, "Go back to your country. The Lord God refused to give me permission to go with you." Balaam failed to tell them that the Israelites could not be cursed because God had blessed them.

As they left, Balaam disappointedly thought, *I am sorry God would not let me go. I would love to have the money King Balak promised me.*

Several weeks later Balaam was surprised when a bigger, more important group of men came pleading. "King Balak begs you to come with us. He promises you great honor. He will pay you whatever you ask. Please come and curse the Israelite people."

Balaam longed to go. But his answer was the same. "Even if King Balak would give me a palace filled with gold and silver, I cannot come unless God lets me. But stay overnight and I shall see what the Lord says." To himself he thought, *Maybe God will change His mind.*

Did Balaam really need to ask God again what he should do? (Discuss.) God had already said enough to him. He must NOT go. Balaam should simply have told the men he could not go with them.

God knew Balaam's heart. He knew that rather than obeying Him, Balaam really wanted money and honor. Instead of doing what God commanded, he wanted to have his own way.

So God said to him, "All right, Balaam, you may go with them. BUT when you get there, you must say ONLY what I tell you to say."

God had not changed His mind. He was simply letting Balaam have his own way.

2. BALAAM GOES TO MOAB
Numbers 22:21-41

The next morning Balaam saddled his donkey and started on the long journey to Moab with the king's messengers. His mind was filled with happy thoughts of the money he would get. He was thinking how important he would be when the king honored him.

It did not bother Balaam that God had not wanted him to go. He was not troubled about the wicked purpose of his trip: to curse God's people.

Balaam's selfish, greedy attitude made God angry. God knew that Balaam would be so eager to receive King Balak's rewards he would forget to say only what God told him. To warn him and also to show Balaam how displeased He was, a miracle was needed.

So God sent an angel with a drawn sword to block the road. Balaam could not see the angel. But his donkey saw him and was so frightened that she bolted off the road. This made Balaam so angry that he hit the donkey.

Farther on, the road went between two walls. Again the donkey saw the angel. To get out of his way, she pressed close to the wall, crushing Balaam's foot. Again Balaam struck the donkey.

The road became extremely narrow. The donkey saw the angel blocking the path. She lay down, making Balaam furious. He whipped the donkey cruelly. Then something miraculous happened. The donkey began to speak! "What have I done that I deserve being beaten?"

"You've made me look like a fool," replied Balaam. He was so angry that he was not even surprised to hear his donkey speak! "If I had my sword, I would kill you!"

"I have served you faithfully for a long time. Have I ever done anything like this before?" asked the donkey.

"No, you have not," Balaam admitted.

Then the Lord opened Balaam's eyes. He saw the angel with his sword drawn to kill him.

Show Illustration #10

Balaam was so scared that he fell on his face before the angel.

Now the angel spoke to him saying, "Why have you beaten your donkey these three times? I came to stop you because you are headed for destruction. Your donkey saw me and tried to avoid me. Otherwise I would have killed you by now."

"I have sinned," Balaam confessed. "I did not know you were here. I will go back home if you do not want me to go on."

"Go on," said the angel. "BUT remember to say *only* what God tells you!"

3. BALAAM BLESSES ISRAEL
Numbers 23, 24

How glad King Balak was to see Balaam! Now his problems would be ended! The next day he took Balaam to the top of a mountain. There he showed him the Israelites camped on the borders of Moab.

Show Illustration #11

Balaam instructed King Balak, "Build seven altars and sacrifice seven bulls and seven rams. You stay here by your offering and I will go to hear what God will say to me."

What do you think God said to Balaam? (Allow discussion.)

When Balaam returned, he said, "King Balak, I cannot curse these people. God has blessed them. Israel is God's special nation."

"Come with me to another place," Balak commanded. "Maybe you can curse some of the Israelites from there."

Again King Balak built seven altars and offered fourteen sacrifices. Balaam went alone to hear what God would say.

Returning, Balaam again gave God's message. "God is not a man. He cannot lie. He does not change His mind as men do. He has promised to bless the people of Israel. He must keep His promise. God has brought them out of Egypt. He has given them unusual strength. They will continue to be victorious. I cannot curse them." King Balak became angry. But Balaam reminded him that he could say only what God told him. Balak tried a third time to get Balaam to curse the Israelites. But God would only let him bless His chosen people.

King Balak became so angry that he shouted, "Balaam, get out of here! Go back home! I called you to curse my enemies, and you just keep blessing them. I was going to promote you to great honor and give you lots of money. But God has kept you from receiving anything!"

4. BALAAM'S ADVICE TO KING BALAK
Numbers 25:1-18; 31:16; Revelation 2:14

"I am sorry, King Balak, that I could not curse these people," Balaam said apologetically. "I wanted to. But God would not let me. I will tell you though how you can defeat these people. Tell the girls of Moab to invite the young men of Israel to their parties. Have them flirt with them and make love to them. Invite the Israelites to your religious feasts when you sacrifice to your idols. Lure them away from their families and from God."

Who gave Balaam such evil advice? (Satan.)

This is exactly what King Balak did. And he succeeded.

Show Illustration #12

Soon the Israelites were not only attending the parties and feasts–they were even bowing down to the idols of the Moabites!

They didn't care that God had commanded them *not* to do this. (See Exodus 20:4-5; 23:24-25, 32-33.) They simply ignored God. (See Exodus 34:16.) They wanted their own way.

Everyone else is doing it. Why must we be different? they thought. *Surely God will not care if we have a little fun.*

But God did care. The Israelites were His special people. He had commanded them to be *holy*–set apart for Himself.

Satan, God's enemy, was happy. He is always glad when God's people are disobedient. BUT God was angry. He sent a plague to the camp of Israel and 24,000 people died! What a high price they paid for having their own way!

And what happened to Balaam? He was slain in battle by the Israelites! The very ones he wanted to curse killed him (Numbers 31:8). God had warned him. The angel had warned him. But he insisted on having his own way and paid with his life!

Let us bow our heads. Quietly think about yourself. Do you really want God's will in your life? Or are you insisting on having your own way? Remember that insisting on our own way brings sorrow and defeat. (See Proverbs 14:12.) Ask God to show you His plan for you. Ask Him to help you follow His will.

Lesson 4
GOD JUDGES MOSES' SIN WITH DEATH

Scripture to be studied: Numbers 20:1-29; 27:12-23; Deuteronomy 3:23-29; 34:1-12

The *aim* of the lesson: To show that when God gives a person much privilege He requires much responsibility.

What your students should *know*: That God may remove His leaders by death when they rebel against His command.

What your students should *feel*: Responsibility to glorify God in their lives.

What your students should *do*: Search their hearts to see if sin is hindering their testimony before others.

Lesson outline (for the teacher's and students' notebooks):
1. Moses tested (Numbers 20:26).
2. Moses fails (Numbers 20:7-29).
3. A new leader appointed (Numbers 27:15-23; Deuteronomy 3:21, 28).
4. Moses dies (Numbers 27:12-14; Deuteronomy 34:1-12).

The verse to be memorized:

God is not a man, that He should lie; neither the son of man, that He should repent: hath He said, and shall He not do it? or hath He spoken and shall He not make it good? (Numbers 23:19)

NOTE TO THE TEACHER

As God's representative to your students, you have an awesome responsibility. You are an example to them. They watch your life. How careful you must be to give glory to God in your words and your actions! You must always practice what you teach. "Unto whom much is given, of him shall much be required" (Luke 12:48).

God deals severely with leaders if their public actions dishonor Him. (See James 3:1.) A leader who sins is a greater stumbling block to others than an ordinary person.

Moses, God's leader, failed to glorify God before the people. Although God forgave him, he had to accept the consequences of his sin. (See Galatians 6:7.) Examine your own life, teacher, as you prepare this lesson. (See Psalm 139:23-24; 19:12b.)

The incident we are now studying has been taken out of its chronological order. It seems wise to combine the account of Moses' death with the reason for it. It did not bother Balaam that God had not wanted him to go. He was not troubled about the wicked purpose of his trip: to curse God's people.

THE LESSON

Did you ever lose a privilege because you were disobedient? Were you kept from going someplace? Or were you not allowed to do something you really wanted to do because you failed to obey?

(Let students give examples from their experiences.)

In our lesson today we are going to learn how God punished one of His superior leaders by withholding a great privilege.

We like to think that God is love, and He is. But God is also strict. As we have seen in the life of Moses, God uses only those who are totally obedient to Him.

(*Teacher:* review the highlights of Moses' life. Question students briefly to help them remember what you have taught.)

Moses was chosen by God from birth to lead the Israelites (Exodus 2).

Moses was miraculously spared as an infant (Exodus 2).

Moses was prepared in Pharaoh's palace (Exodus 2).

Moses was courageous before Pharaoh (Exodus 5-12).

Moses' leadership of Israel:
  Out of Egypt (Exodus 12:31–14:31).
  Through the wilderness (choose some incidents).
  Spokesman for God.

Moses had the privilege of meeting God face-to-face, receiving messages directly from Him (Exodus 20; 33:11).

Moses was looking forward to entering the land God had promised His people. For 40 years Moses had been a faithful leader. His task had not been easy. What a trial the people had been! They continually complained. They rebelled against God. They grumbled against Moses. Over and over again Moses had fallen on his face before God to pray for them. Each time God had heard and answered him.

1. MOSES TESTED
Numbers 20:26

The time came when the Israelite people camped at a place called Meribah-Kadesh. Miriam died here and was buried. (Review briefly the highlights of Miriam's life.)

Then there was a problem. The people had no water. Coming to Moses they said, "We cannot find any water to drink. There is no water for our animals. Nor can we wash our clothes."

Think what a serious problem you'd have if there was no water in your town or village. No one can live long without water.

The Israelites began to complain. Their grumbling turned into anger. Almost two million thirsty people were crying for water.

The leaders came to Moses. They were bitter. "We wish we had died here in the wilderness with our parents! Why did you bring us out of Egypt? This is an evil place. We hate it here. There is nothing to eat, and we have no water to drink."

Does this sound familiar? They were accusing Moses of the same things their parents had. Many of these people had been children when their parents could not find water. Do you remember how God provided water for them at Rephidim almost 38 years before? (Review Exodus 17:1-7.)

What should the people have done? (Let students answer. They should have turned humbly to God telling Him their need.) Instead of thanking God for His goodness to them, they angrily asked, "Is the Lord among us or not?"

They could see the answer to that question. The cloud was still over them by day. The pillar of fire could still be seen at night. Every morning there was manna to eat.

Poor Moses! How discouraged he felt as he listened to their complaints! The Bible does not tell us what he thought. But could it have been something like this? *Haven't these people learned anything after 40 long years? Don't they know God cares for them?*

Moses could have called a group of the leaders together to decide what to do. He could have sent out search parties to find water. What do you think he did? (Let students respond.)

Show Illustration #13

As before, Moses fell on his face and prayed. He knew that God was the only One who could supply water for thousands in a desert.

If we had been in God's place, we would have given up long before with such complaining people. But God is patient. Once again He told Moses what to do. Pointing to a nearby rock, God instructed, "Moses, take your rod. Call the leaders together. SPEAK to the rock before their eyes. Water will flow out of the rock. There will be plenty for all the people and their animals."

How did this command differ from the one 38 years before at Rephidim? *(This time Moses was to SPEAK to the rock, not STRIKE it.)*

2. MOSES FAILS
Numbers 20:7-29

Moses gathered the people together before the rock. Then angrily he called out, "Listen, you rebels! Must *we* bring you water out of this rock?"

Show Illustration #14

While everyone watched, Moses lifted his rod and *struck* the rock twice. And streams of water gushed out–plenty for all the people and their animals.

But what was wrong with Moses' action? (Let students answer.)

(1) He lost his temper. (2) He spoke as though *he*–instead of God–was going to provide the water. (3) He struck the rock instead of speaking to it. (4) He struck the rock twice.

God was angry with Moses. (See Deuteronomy 1:37.) "Moses," He scolded, "you have done wrong. You did not *believe* me. You are the leader of My people. They follow your example. You disobeyed Me. You neither gave glory to nor honored Me before My people. Because of your sin, you may not lead My people into the land I promised them. You will die here in the wilderness!"

What a disappointment! Perhaps you think God was too strict with Moses. Maybe you think Moses' sin was not as big as the sins of the Israelites. God often withheld His punishment from them.

But Moses was God's spokesman to the people. He was their leader. When the one in charge sins, everyone knows it. A leader has great influence on many people. Those who observe him think, *If he can do that, so can I.* How careful leaders must be always! They must honor God so others will think well of Him. (See Luke 12:48.)

Maybe you are thinking, *I am not a leader so this does not apply to me.* Are you a Christian? Then it does apply to you. You are representing Christ. Others are watching you. Do others want to belong to Christ because of the way you live? Or do they say, "If that is what a Christian is, I do not want to be one." God will hold you responsible for the way you live. (See Romans 14:10-12.)

The weeks went by. One day God said to Moses, "It is time for Aaron to die. Like you, he will not go into the land because you both rebelled against Me at Meribah-Kadesh when you struck the rock. Take Aaron and his son, Eleazar, up the mountain. Remove Aaron's high priestly garments and put them on Eleazar." The people watched as the three men climbed out of sight. When Moses and Eleazar returned, Aaron was not with them. Eleazar stood before the people as their new high priest.

3. A NEW LEADER APPOINTED
Numbers 27:15-23; Deuteronomy 3:21, 28

Moses loved the Israelites. He had been their leader a long time. He knew they could never get along without a strong leader.

Again he turned to God. "O God," he prayed, "before I die, please appoint a new leader for the people. Give them a man who will guide them. Choose someone to care for them so they will not be like sheep without a shepherd."

God answered Moses, saying, "Go get Joshua. Bring him before Eleazar the priest." What do you remember about Joshua? (Review incident of spies, Numbers 14.)

God continued, "Gather all the people together. Let them watch as you lay your hands on Joshua and turn over your authority to him. Let them hear as you charge him with the responsibility of leading My people. All the people will know that Joshua is to be their leader. They must obey him."

Show Illustration #15

It was not easy for Moses to give his position to another. But he obeyed God. He laid his hands on Joshua, setting him apart as God's servant. He encouraged Joshua saying, "Do not be afraid of the nations over in the land God has promised us. Remember, the Lord God will fight for you. Be strong. Be courageous. You will lead the people into their new homeland. God will be with you. He will never fail you." (See Deuteronomy 3:22; 31:6, 8, 23.)

4. MOSES DIES
Numbers 27:12-14; Deuteronomy 34:1-12

Moses really wanted to go into the land with the people. This had been his hope for forty years. He pleaded with God, "Please, O Lord God, let me go over and see the good land beyond the Jordan River."

God's answer was not what Moses wanted to hear. "No, Moses, you may not enter Canaan. Do not ask Me again!"

Moses had confessed his sin. He knew he had disobeyed. He did not try to defend himself. God had forgiven Moses. But he had to suffer the consequences of his sin.

When Moses was 120 years old, his life was almost finished. But first he had a farewell message for the people of Israel. He reminded them of God's faithfulness. He reviewed God's rules. He warned them of God's punishment for disobedience. This is all recorded in the Book of Deuteronomy which we shall study next.

Show Illustration #16

After this, God took Moses to the top of Mount Pisgah. (Indicate on map. Nebo and Pisgah are two peaks of the Abarim mountain ranges.) From there Moses could see the promised land of Canaan stretched before him. God spoke to him saying, "This is the land which I promised to Abraham, Isaac and Jacob, and to their children."

Then Moses died and God buried him. Not one person knew where he was buried.

Listen to what God said about Moses. "And there arose not a prophet since in Israel like unto Moses, whom the Lord knew face to face" (Deuteronomy 34:10). What a wonderful testimony! What will God say about you?

We all feel sad that Moses could not go into the land. But this should be a warning to us. Sometimes people think God will not care if they sin. They believe they can live as they please and God will forgive them when they confess their sins. God *will* forgive. But many times, like a good father, He punishes His children. (See Galatians 6:7.)

One thing more: we will never be too old to sin. Therefore, we must walk close to the Lord every day.

Let us bow our heads together. Ask God to show you any sin in your life which spoils your testimony before others. Ask God to help you to live every day so He will be glorified and honored before others.